Praying with Posture

Short Meditations for the Whole Body

Gina Hall

Praying with Posture
Published by **Redemptorist Publications**
A Registered Charity limited by guarantee. Registered in England 3261721.

First published March 2009

Cover design and illustrations by Chris Nutbeen
Layout by Rosemarie Pink

Photographs used by kind permission of Gina Hall

ISBN 978-0-85231-360-2

A CIP catalogue record for this book is available from the British Library

Printed by Joseph Ball Limited, Leicester LE2 5LQ

Alphonsus House Chawton Hampshire GU34 3HQ
Telephone 01420 88222   01420 88805
rp@rpbooks.co.uk   www.rpbooks.co.uk

This book uses pictures of crosses and calvaries as the focus for a series of six meditations on the physical postures of worship and devotion, and relates these to the life of Jesus. The wayside cross is a common sight in France and other parts of mainland Europe.

Begin each meditation with the recommended Bible passage. Take time to read the scripture slowly. Be quiet and peaceful, and allow even familiar words and phrases to deliver their full meaning. Adopt the attitude for each meditation; explore how it feels.

You might set aside time each day for a different meditation, or use one section over a whole week, taking time to reread the Bible passage, and repeat the posture and meditation.

Let the words, the feeling of the posture, and the picture of the cross take you on your personal journey.

1

Sitting or kneeling with head bowed

Read

Luke 1 and 2

The story of Zechariah and Elizabeth, and the birth of John the Baptist; the annunciation; the birth of Jesus; Jesus' childhood.

I bow my head.

I feel the muscles stretch down my neck, right down my back. I look down and I am not distracted by the things all around me. My eyes see only the page of meditation, the shrine arched, like a bowed body.

I think of the many heads that have bowed in devotion and prayer over all the years. Zechariah, bowed in the Temple, Elizabeth bowed in thankful prayer, Mary bowed in acceptance of God's will.

I think of Mary, head bowed, cradling the infant Jesus. I think how that would feel – to bow, not only before God, but around God. I take time to cradle God, to experience God within my bowed form. I think of the unborn Jesus: curled, bowed in the womb; Joseph bowed to deliver the child; shepherds and wise men bowed in devotion.

I bow before God and around God. I feel the muscles of my body, the body created by God. I feel the muscles and the bones of my body doing my will.

I offer myself to do God's will.

2

Sitting with your hands together

Read

Mark 1:16-45 and 2:1-12

The calling of the disciples; Jesus heals many who are sick.

I hold my hands together.

I feel the palms one against another. I feel the skin, the flesh, and the bones underneath. I think of all the people who have pressed their hands together in prayer.

I think of the hands of Jesus holding the tools of the carpenter, feeling the wood. I look at the wooden cross, made by the hands of a carpenter, now weathered and rough. I think of the hands of Simon and Andrew: rough hands of fishermen, strong hands to pull nets, hands chapped from wet and wind.

I think of the hands of Jesus reaching out to heal, stretching out to heal, touching to heal, holding a hand to heal.

I feel those holding, healing hands touching me, enclosing my two hands in his hands.

I think of the hands that dug through the roof, opening a way to lower a friend to Jesus. I look at my hands, pressed together, and I think of those hands dirty from digging, aching and sore: hands that have dug through the roof of a building to reach God. I think of the hands of the paralysed man as he picked up his mat: hands that have dragged a paralysed body; hands that couldn't do their proper work; hands that now hold the mat, doing the bidding of Jesus.

I feel my hands and I offer them to do God's will.

3

Sitting or kneeling with
your hands open

Read

Matthew 3; 5:1-19 and
6:7-15

*The proclamation of John;
the baptism of Jesus; Jesus
teaching on the mountain.*

I hold my hands open.

I look at my hands, at the lines and the creases, the knuckles
and palms. I think of the hands of John – the hands of a
strong man, the hands of a bold man. Hands that draw the
faithful believer into the water, hands that raise the believer
up again renewed.

I think of the hands of Jesus raised in praise and acceptance
as he rises from the baptismal water. I hear the water
dripping from those hands and see the light sparkling in
the droplets.

I look at my hands; I think of the things they do: good things,
working things, wrong things, beautiful things.

I think of Jesus teaching: hands raised, open, illustrating a
point. I think of Jesus praying: hands raised and open. Jesus
teaching us to pray. Jesus teaching us to accept God's will,
to ask, to forgive.

I look at my hands. I thank God for the things they can do,
I ask forgiveness for the wrong things I have used them for,
and I offer them to God to do God's will.

4

Kneeling

Read

John 12:1-8 and 13:1-38

Mary anoints Jesus' feet with perfume; Jesus washes his disciples' feet.

I kneel.

I feel the ground beneath my bent knees; I feel the muscles through my body. I feel my legs bend under me, my back holding me. I think of the thousands who have knelt through the years, lowering themselves, curving themselves, coming before God humbly, in stillness and quiet.

I think of Mary kneeling at the feet of Jesus, kneeling low to touch his feet. Kneeling low to the ground in acceptance of who Jesus is. Kneeling low to worship him, kneeling low to wash his feet, perfume his feet, dry his feet with her hair. Kneeling so low in the beauty of selfless devotion. I think of the feet of Jesus: feet used to walking; dusty; tired feet, feet that would be pierced with the nails of crucifixion.

I think of Jesus kneeling at the feet of his friends, his disciples. I imagine the water pouring into the bowl, the sound, the sight of the water catching the light as it flows. I think of Jesus kneeling, his knees bent like mine, his body folded, curved like mine. He lifts those feet: tired, dusty feet. He pours water; and uses his hands to wash away the dust and dirt. He takes the towel and dries the feet. He moves, kneels again, pours and washes, and dries. Do the disciples do this humble service for each other? Do I? I set aside my pride, my self-importance, my power and position. I come humbly to God.

I offer myself to selfless service, to kneel, to be low to wash the feet of others.

5

Sitting or standing with your arms open wide

Read

Luke 23 and John 19

Jesus before Pilate and Herod; Jesus' crucifixion and burial.

I stand with my arms open wide.

I feel the muscles in my shoulders, my back and my arms. I think of arms held wide in praise, and arms held wide in the suffering of the cross. I think of the people who had held up their hands to praise Jesus as he rode into Jerusalem.

Were some of those who raised their arms in praise the same people who raised their hands to shout for the death of Jesus? I think of the crossroads, the choices in my life: do I consistently choose God, or do I choose my own path?

I think of the arms of Jesus, open on the cross, dying and yet embracing: embracing the crucified criminal who repents, accepting him into paradise.

The arms of Jesus open on the cross, dying yet embracing: embracing Mary his mother, providing her with a son, and the young man whom he loved with a mother. The arms of Jesus open on the cross, dying yet embracing: embracing me.

I think of the strain and the pain, the anguish and the agony.

I think of the love.

I think of arms open in suffering, open in glory, open in resurrection.

I open my arms; I embrace God's will; I embrace God's call for my life. I embrace those whom God would have me embrace. I open my arms in worship.

13

6

Choose a posture; a
movement; a stillness
that you want to bring to
worship and meditation

Read

Luke 24 and John 20

*Jesus is resurrected and
appears to his disciples.*

I breathe in and out and I feel my lungs expand. I think of
Jesus breathing in resurrected life.

I bow my face to the ground as the women did at the tomb.
I weep with Mary. I allow the feeling of loss, the loss of my
Lord, so that I may embrace the feeling of gain. I am brought
low in the fear I should have in the face of God who is more
powerful than death.

I run with the excitement of the risen Jesus, feeling the air
rush past me, my body alive with movement.

I walk with the disciples on the road to Emmaus. As I walk,
I walk with the risen Jesus. I share the ease of walking in his
company.

I sit with the risen Jesus; familiar food and drink are on the
table. I find fresh pleasure in the acts of taking food, eating
food, sharing food.

I allow the presence of Jesus into the room with me. I open
my heart to his presence. I allow him to open my mind to
understand the scriptures. I accept his blessing, offered to
me, his hands raised, my hands raised.

The Wayside Calvary

The calvaries that illustrate this book are all from "my" part of France: the Mayenne; a quiet, unspoilt region south of Normandy, and inland from Brittany. For me it is a place to retreat from everyday life, a place for quiet, for meditation, and for time to be closer to God.

All across the region, as in most parts of France, the roads are punctuated with a wayside cross, or a calvary, or a shrine. For hundreds of years families and communities have placed these structures along the roads, sometimes at the entrance to a farm or group of houses, sometimes at a crossroads, or just at a spot by the roadside. The forms are as varied as humanity's ingenuity; early crosses, many of which date from the seventeenth century, are carved in stone, often with naive representations of the crucified Christ carved into the surface. Later variations take advantage of mass-produced cast-iron figures applied to wooden crosses. Then there are shrines with a space for flowers and holy figures; and simple wooden crosses, handmade from local oak, growing weathered with the years. Occasionally a modern example appears in steel tubing or bright colours, or lit up at night.

They are, and have always been, places for private devotion, places to pause, to think, to remember. When placed at crossroads the symbolism is hard to miss – which path should I take in my life, as in my journey? I often make my own pilgrimage along the quiet lanes, with time to meditate, and every few kilometres a cross, a focus for my thoughts, a place for prayer.